"Kyle has written a very timely and necessary work addressing our attachment to social media. Without throwing the baby out with the bathwater, Kyle challenges the Christian to a God-honoring approach to social media involvement. Well researched and thought through, Unfriend Yourself avoids the emotional arguments and instead presents a provocative 'must read' for any students, young adults, and generations beyond who want to be responsible in approaching social media from a biblical worldview. This book will make you think! Thanks, Kyle, for this much needed, practical, and contemplative work."

Dr. Bob MacRae
Professor of Youth Ministry
Moody Bible Institute

"With Unfriend Yourself Kyle strikes a resonate chord with his generation and provides needed leadership through the wonders and warnings of social media relationships. Kyle's compelling research and personal insight successfully equip the reader with an effective biblical framework through which to address the growing place social media is taking in our daily lives. Embrace Kyle's relevant and thought-provoking challenge, and find yourself better off for it."

Brian Kammerzelt
Communications Department Chair
Moody Bible Institute

D1446423

unfriend
yourself

unfriend
yourself

THREE DAYS TO DETOX, DISCERN,

AND DECIDE ABOUT SOCIAL MEDIA

KYLE TENNANT

MOODY PUBLISHERS
CHICAGO

Scripture quotations are taken from *The Holy Bible, English Standard Version.*
Copyright © 2000, 2001 by Crossway Bibles, a division of Good News Publishers.
Used by permission. All rights reserved.

Edited by Brandon O'Brien

Cover design: Kathryn Joachim

Interior design: Smart Guys design

Library of Congress Cataloging-in-Publication Data
Tennant, Kyle.
 Unfriend yourself : three days to detox, discern, and decide about social
media / by Kyle Tennant.
    p. cm.
 Includes bibliographical references.
 ISBN 978-0-8024-0953-9
1. Social media. 2. Online social networks. 3. Interpersonal relations. I. Title.
 HM742.T46 2012
 302.23'1--dc23

                    2011043190

All websites and phone numbers listed herein are accurate at the time of publication,
but may change in the future or cease to exist. The listing of website references
and resources does not imply publisher endorsement of the site's entire contents.
Groups and organizations are listed for informational purposes, and listing does not
imply publisher endorsement of their activities.

We hope you enjoy this book from Moody Publishers. Our goal is to provide high-
quality, thought-provoking books and products that connect truth to your real needs
and challenges. For more information on other books and products written and
produced from a biblical perspective, go to www.moodypublishers.com or write to:

Moody Publishers
820 N. LaSalle Boulevard
Chicago, IL 60610

3 5 7 9 10 8 6 4 2

Printed in the United States of America

To my professors,
who taught me how to think

Contents

Introduction

My name is Kyle, and over a year ago, I said farewell to Facebook. Well, at least I tried.

It all started in a class. (How often do we start stories like that?) I wanted to study how Christians and churches should use Facebook, so for my independent study course I planned to write a paper called "The Application of Social Media in the Local Church." At the time, I was going to a rather net-savvy church and wanted to explore more fully how we could use these new technologies.

Then I met with my professor. Only a few years older than me and well-versed in the goings-on of communication theory, he seemed like the perfect fit. Except for when he told me that I was asking the wrong question. I was asking, "*How* should the church be using social media?" My professor kindly removed that first word, and in so doing, launched me on a journey that would change the way I think about the world. It's funny how changing one little word, *how*, could do so much.

So I began my study, seeking to answer my new question, "Should the church be using social media at all?" To answer this question, I had to create a new reading list. Instead of reading only works fresh off the presses of Christian publishing houses everywhere, I started reading works by authors who had been buried over a decade ago. Instead of only reading books on ministry practice, I started reading communications theory and texts on sociology, technology, and culture. While I did spend a significant amount of time reading contemporary works, I started with the dead guys, who provided me the framework to understand the newer stuff.

Before I knew it, the project was practically running away from me. I could barely keep up with the unending flow of data found in books, journal articles, magazines, newspapers, and, of course, blogs. Soon the magnum opus of my undergraduate career emerged: a ten thousand word essay on the dangers and ills of social media.

I started as someone eagerly following the latest social media trends. One semester later, I started to wonder if I should be using social media at all. I wanted to unfriend myself.

Now let's be clear: I have a Facebook account, and I check it three to five times daily (becoming a youth pastor kind of forced my hand, but we'll talk about that later). I'm no stranger to Twitter (I tweet less than once a week—I find it an interesting experiment in networking), and I do occasionally blog. So I have not given up on social media entirely (more on that later, too). But what I have come to see is that one of the dominant cultural metaphors of our time is not to be trusted, nor is it to be lauded. In fact, it may be our generation's greatest enemy. Okay, so maybe that's exaggerating—but the point is that social media may do far more damage to our relationships, and our understanding of them, than we may think. Though social media promise us relationships and community, they may in truth be promising us a lie.

In essence, that is what this book explores. In the following pages, I will take you on the same journey I have been on for the last year or so, offering you everything I have read and thought on the subject. In so doing, I hope to evaluate the claims social media have made about us and our society, and hopefully debunk some of them. In *Unfriend Yourself*, I also hope you and I will learn to go beyond the social media options to deepen and appreciate true friendships.

This book is designed to be read over a weekend—though you don't have to do it that way, I'd really encourage it. The book is also designed to be read while you are taking three days off from your favorite social network—probably Face-book. It's a time to detox. It's time for a weekend—and maybe longer—to unfriend yourself from your favorite social media.

In some ways, this book becomes a guided "Facebook fast," taking the time you would be spending updating your status and posting photos and replacing it with reading this book. I promise, Scout's honor, that you can read each chapter in under an hour, even if you are a bit of a slow reader.

At the end of every chapter, you'll find a few action steps to take, like writing your best friend a letter, or finding some-one to hug (you'll see). These action steps are also part of the whole *Unfriend Yourself* experience; they are my attempt at helping you immediately apply what you are reading.

By the end of the book, it's my hope that you will have gained a basic understanding of communication theory and have thought through what those theories mean on a theological level—hence, discern. In the final chapter, I will offer some of the tools necessary to help you figure out what to do when you log on come Monday morning—you'll decide.

So, before you turn to chapter 1, cut the umbilical cord. Unfriend yourself, and say farewell for the weekend. Don't worry, the world can wait; your "friends" won't even know you're gone—seriously, there are over half a billion Facebook users out there. I doubt you'll be missed.

Have you done it?

No?

How about now?

You have. Good.

Now turn the page, and enjoy your Friday.

detox

The first time Facebook failed me was in my senior year of high school, though I really didn't know it until my first year of college. (In fact, I didn't fully understand the significance of this failure until I began the research that resulted in this book.) When I was a high school senior, Facebook was still relatively new; in fact, the powers-that-be had only recently opened the site to high school students and people without .edu email addresses. I found Facebook to be a fun way to spend a few minutes online after school. This was before apps, chat, or even "likes" came to be, so Facebook was not nearly the time vacuum it is today.

In February of 2007, I was accepted to the college of my dreams, Moody Bible Institute. A few months later, I logged onto Facebook to discover an invitation to the "Moody Bible

Institute Class of 2011" Facebook group. This glimpse into my future, provided by dozens of gleaming profiles of my soon-to-be-classmates, became a balmy oasis in the midst of my senioritis-induced boredom.

I'd been experiencing symptoms of senioritis since my sophomore year of high school; by the time I began my senior year I could barely stand to sit in my high school any longer. I desperately wanted to shuffle off the coil of my Midwestern high school and flee to Chicago where, I was sure, a better life awaited me. So imagine my delight upon discovering this digital invitation awaiting me at home one afternoon. I immediately accepted and plunged into a world of exciting new friendships. I would spend hours on Facebook writing back and forth with my newfound "friends."

At first, most of our communication was the typical get-to-know you stuff: hometown, interests, intended major at Moody, dreams for our futures. Soon, however, it turned into something far more personal. Someone created a discussion board or two for us to share prayer requests and our testimonies. The two dozen or so of us using the group regularly hailed this as a great idea. Soon we were sharing the wounded parts of ourselves with each other; we found great comfort and encouragement during those weeks and months, written in friendly Facebook font.

Like I mentioned, there were only about two dozen of us using the group with any regularity—the other hundred or so tended to use it to ask the few upperclassmen who had joined what to bring or not to bring, which classes to take or not to take, and so on. That's if they used it at all. I remember feeling bad for the majority of people who weren't using the group to what I saw as its potential. I think the two dozen true users all felt that we were getting a running start on our social lives via Facebook. I was investing in friendships that, I was sure, would become the most treasured of my life.

As it turned out, I was wrong.

We moved onto campus on a clear, sunny Chicago day in late August. As I stood in lines waiting to get my keys and the signatures of various officials around campus, I saw familiar faces—those who had posted their Facebook photos over the summer. Yet very few of us approached each other that day to say hello. And when someone did come to greet me, a funny thing happened: we didn't know what to do. Should we hug, or just shake hands? Being the kind of guy who hugs, I considered this a serious question. I hug my friends when I see them, so was I supposed to hug my Facebook friends now that I was meeting them in person?

It got stranger. As we met in person, we were confronted by the strangest questions: do we introduce ourselves as if we'd never met, or were we to greet each other as old friends? Were we to skip the details we already knew—hometown, major, struggles, and heartaches—or were we to start over and discuss them like it was the first time we'd heard such news? *When I met my Facebook friends in the flesh, I found that our exchanges were not easier but more difficult.* They were awkward and stiff. Our first conversations, of the get-to-know-you kind we all use to start relationships, were derailed, short-circuited.

Fast forward a few years, and my college career is over. In my four years studying at Moody, I met some of my best friends. We walked through many hard things together and struggled together through many griefs; we also had many shared joys and fun moments. However, none of the people who played a significant role in my life on Facebook *before* coming to college played a significant role in my life *during* college.

It seems that, while I truly believed I was becoming a part of these people's lives via Facebook, I wasn't. Many of the people I "got to know" on Facebook are little more than acquaintances now and weren't much more during our first semester. Today, all of those with whom I'd shared my life via social media are not my friends. They were never the people intimately involved in my life, despite the things I told them online. Oddly enough, it is the people I "friended" on Facebook, but with whom I interacted little electronically, that I am closest with today.

In hindsight, this chapter in my life displays how social media were and are offering more than they can deliver. It was reflecting on this experience as I started studying and reading and writing that helped me confirm that there was something not quite right about social media and the way we use them.

Don't Be a Hater

As I write, I am only weeks away from graduation, a twenty-three-year-old about to enter the "real world." I started a Facebook profile in high school, and continue to maintain it. Most often, I check Facebook and other social media from my phone. I have been known to use Twitter, and I occasionally blog (I say "occasionally" because I rarely have the necessary discipline to keep it going with any regularity).

What I'm trying to say is that I am one of you, one of you college-aged social media users who make up a hefty portion of social media's clientele. I have grown up on Facebook and grown up online. I am not an outside observer to social media and technology; I am a native. My concerns have grown while living inside the digital bubble, and even with those concerns I have chosen to remain inside of the bubble. Condemnation rarely changes anything.

In other words, this is not a book about how Facebook is evil; it is a book about thinking. Writing in 1963, Harry Blamires

an Age of Entertainment was written by Neil Postman in the 1980s. His work came alongside another similar work, *Understanding Media: Extensions of Man* by Marshall McLuhan, who coined the famous (though mysterious) adage, "The medium is the message."

This is an often-used and little-understood phrase. But when I came to see what McLuhan, and then Postman, meant by it, everything began to make sense. The medium is the message means that

> in the long run a medium's content matters less than the medium itself in influencing how we think and act. As our window onto the world, and onto ourselves, a popular medium molds what we see and how we see it—and eventually, if we use it enough, it changes who we are, as individuals and as a society.[5]

Postman wrote that every medium has resonance.[6] That is, a medium's power and influence resonates—echoes, grows, increases—in ways that we can't quite predict. In the end, a medium changes the way we think and the way we relate; a medium has creative power that extends far beyond itself. "A medium is the social and intellectual environment a machine creates," he says.[7] Media have a peculiar power to shape and change us as we use them and they use us. Media have great effect on us because they are "intellectual technologies." "It is our intellectual technologies that have the greatest and most lasting power over what and how we think," writes Nicholas Carr. He says that intellectual technologies

> are our most intimate tools, the ones we use for self-expression and for shaping personal and public identity, and for cultivating relations with others . . . when [intellectual technologies] come into popular use, [they] often promote new ways of thinking or extend to the general population established ways of thinking that had been limited to a small, elite group.[8]

So back to the promise Facebook makes, or more appropriately, that technology makes as a whole. We have come to believe that how we communicate doesn't really matter; we think that media are neutral vehicles, well under our control. We believe that social media are our tools, and that these tools are our friends. As Carr notes,

> In the end, we come to pretend that the technology itself doesn't matter. It's how we use it that matters, we tell ourselves. The implication, comforting in its hubris, is that we're in control. The technology is just a tool, inert until we pick it up and inert again once we set it aside.[9]

We are wrong. A medium is not a neutral bystander in our communication. Quite the opposite: "Every technology has an inherent bias," writes Postman. "It has within its physical form a predisposition toward being used in certain ways and not others. Only those who know nothing of the history of technology believe that a technology is entirely neutral . . . Each technology has an agenda of its own."[10] Media desire, ever so subtly, to be used in certain ways to the exclusion of others. Take television, for example. Postman's work dealt largely with the shift from a culture built on the written word to a culture built on the televised world. "Entertainment," he wrote, "is the supra-ideology of all discourse on television."[11] In essence, whatever you put into television comes out the other side as entertainment. Whether it be a cartoon, an evening drama, or even the morning news, television's agenda is to make everything into entertainment. The television's agenda is the laugh.

Of course, there are some instances in which the use of a medium can escape the agenda: "After all, it is not unheard of that a format will occasionally go against the bias of its medium."[12] For example, the Sunday morning news program *Meet the Press* is a very thoughtful, information-packed program that doesn't seek to entertain us, but to inform us. Implied in Postman's comment is that it is the exception, not the norm, for information generated through a medium to go against the very nature of that medium. The agenda of a medium is very difficult, indeed, to circumvent. As we use media, they shape intellectual and social ecosystems that in turn shape the way we see the world.

Instead of being neutral bystanders to our everyday lives, Facebook and its compatriots have an agenda, a way that they want to be used. Every time we log on we are participating in the creative power of the medium; our use of Facebook is changing the way we see the world and how we interact with each other. Our use of social media is creating an intellectual, and more importantly, social environment in which we all live, move, and breathe.

Promise 2: It's okay to make it all about you.
When we move online to Facebook and other social media, we find that these technologies, too, have their own agendas. Where the supra-ideology (or controlling set of values) of television is entertainment, the supra-ideology of social media is *me.* In essence, Facebook's agenda is for us to broadcast ourselves (notably the YouTube tagline), to talk about what we're doing and what we like. This is what psychologists might call "self-presentation," which is a fancy psychological word for what we do all the time: we wear clothes, talk in a certain way, do things how we do them, all to tell the world about who we are. Facebook is a digital opportunity for us to self-present through status updates, photos, and "likes."

The problem with the promise comes when we realize that:

Self-Presentation

+ Sinful Selves

= Self-Promotion

When we step into our digital lives, we suddenly find that instead of passively or thoughtlessly telling people about ourselves (like we do in casual conversation, or with our clothing), we are sending to the world constant and premeditated messages about the details of our lives. We present—or promote—ourselves in such a way to cause people to think of us in a certain way. When I log on to Facebook, I find that I want to put my best foot forward; as a result, I find myself bending the truth and skirting circumstance, ever so slightly, to offer to my "friends" the best part of myself, the part of me that is the coolest, the funniest. I announce to others something good about me with the goal of getting others to think a certain way about me. The biblical term for this kind of self-promotion is "boasting."

But what goes around comes around. "By showcasing the most witty, joyful, bullet-pointed versions of people's lives, and inviting constant comparisons in which we tend to see ourselves as the losers, Facebook appears to exploit an Achilles' heel of human nature."[13] As I "stalk" the profiles of my "friends," I find that they, too, have put their best foot forward; and tragically, I don't measure up. Suddenly, I think to myself: "Oh, I'm not nearly as fit as he is," or "She is far more witty than I am." As a result, I want to find ways to make myself look better so that I can keep up with everyone else. So begins an endless cycle of self-promotion and self-rejection.[14]

Quite frankly, it's exhausting, running on this hamster wheel of the approval of others; and I am almost positive that I am not the only one to have experienced this.

Facebook has a tendency to inflame a condition we already have (striking our aforementioned Achilles' heel): thinking of ourselves more highly than we ought to think. Facebook, Twitter, and other social media provide us with unhindered opportunities to distribute information about ourselves to mass amounts of people very quickly. The problem is that this information is often trivial and inane, which subtly teaches us that the inane details of our lives are important for other people to know.

Before we know it, our way of thinking has changed. We broadcast everything to everyone all of the time, and con-sider this normal and acceptable. A quick look on Facebook tells me that a "friend" has four tickets to a concert he wants to give away, that another got pulled over last night, that another hates spiders. Facebook and social media tell us that the endlessly inane and mindless details of our lives are newsworthy (notice Facebook calls it a "news feed"). But this promise is a lie.

I am not the center of the universe, and the funny thing my friend's cat just did is not all that important. Sure, there is a laugh to be had, but ever so subtly we have come to believe that everything about me matters, when it truly doesn't. Boasting, self-promotion, and self-construction are dangerous habits of the mind and heart.

Promise 3: Community can be found anywhere.

Facebook offers us convenience and ease when it comes to friendship and community. Quality time with friends used to be spent over coffee or dinner. Now more and more of our community life is managed digitally. Some studies show that most people communicate more online than they do offline.[15]

Remember that a medium creates a social environment. This is exactly what is happening. We go to Facebook only to build community, rather than maintain it. This was my goal when I was seeking out so many people on Facebook before going away to school—I was seeking to build a community. Yet this project failed.

Attempts to build a true community online will always fail, because you are using the tool for a task the designer didn't have in mind. It's like using a screwdriver to cut down a tree. In the early days, we called Facebook and other similar sites "social networks," but now we call them "online communities." As *networks*, the sites operated on clearer boundaries.

Carr concludes, "The interactivity of the medium has also turned it into the world's meetinghouse, where people gather to chat, gossip, argue, show off, and flirt on Facebook, Twitter, MySpace, and all sorts of other social (and sometimes antisocial) networks."[16]

Somewhere, somehow, networks and communities became one and the same. Networks, intended for touch-point, shallow relationships based on a single affinity, became communities, intended for authenticity, intimacy, and all-of-life affinity. What we find is that "we are changed as technology offers us substitutes for connecting with each other face-to-face."[17]

Unlike a network, which is built on communication, community is built on communion. "Too often we applaud technologies that enable us to exchange information (communication) without attending to those means of sharing that build intimacy and deepen our communion with God and each other."[18] Communication is easy. A simple text is communication, but it is not communion. A wall post is communication, but it is not communion.

Communion is constructed from two simple, yet profound, elements: orality and presence. Orality is "our speaking and listening 'in person' with each other."[19] Presence is physical, in-the-flesh togetherness. Notice, though, that both of these elements dwindle in the world of social media. You may have one (typically orality) but never both. Suddenly, these building blocks are removed, and instead of communing, we are only communicating.

While we would like to believe social media offer us opportunities for friendship, community, and communion, we ask too much. This, perhaps, is a promise Facebook never intended to propagate and we have forced upon it. After all, according to the website and tagline, Facebook only promises opportunities to *connect* with friends.

The truth is, community—true community, where we find intimacy and authenticity—requires a lot more than a simple message. Yet, we are easily deceived, and we easily accept off-brand community when we should be partaking of the real deal.

Promise 4: Nowhere is somewhere, and it can be anywhere.
Remember that while orality may continue when we go online, our presence disappears. We leave our bodies behind, and step into a place that is not a place, a world that is not a world. Social media tell us that we can be anywhere, even miles apart from our loved ones, and still be intimate with them. We can meet them "online," which we consider a "there" and "place" and find community. But the problem is that "there" is nowhere at all.

A funny thing happens, though, when we conceive of the digital world as just that, a *world.* "When part of your life is lived in virtual places—it can be Second Life, a computer game, a social networking site—a vexed relationship develops between what is true and what is 'true here,' true in simulation."[20] A strange kind of seeping happens when we live more and more of our lives online. What is acceptable *there,* in Facebook or Twitter, becomes acceptable *here,* in real life.

Facebook and social media teach us, subtly, that our bodies don't matter. We can abandon presence and spend more and more time online. Sure, we spend time together, but not really; we spend time "together," online, in chat rooms, and in texting conversations. This, however, is a problem, for

> if you're spending three, four, or five hours a day in an online game or virtual world [or a social media site] . . . there's got to be somewhere you're not. And that someplace you're not is often with your family and friends—sitting around, playing Scrabble face-to-face, taking a walk, watching a movie together in the old-fashioned way.[21]

As we are robbed of our bodies, and presence is eviscerated from our friendships, we face a tragic loss: we are no longer face to face, but screen to screen. We become mediated (note the first five letters, *media*). Yet "the best relationships we can have are *not* those that rely on mediation, but rather the ones that allow for *unmediated* contact and communication."[22]

We seem to have an innate sense that being in the flesh is more meaningful than being mediated over Skype or Facebook or the telephone. I left home in 2007 to go to college, and I frequently returned home. Why? Because unmediated communication—*communion face to face*—is innately better than mediated communication. If we really believed that mediated communication makes no difference to our relationships, and if we really believed that unmediated quality time and mediated communication were really one and the same, why do we go home from college?

We go home because we know that dwelling bodily with one another is the best kind of relationship, and that playing Scrabble and going on walks and having long conversations over coffee and playing Frisbee in the yard is far preferable to being apart. While social media may have tried to teach us differently (and with some success), we have to remember that our bodies matter and that true communion is found when we are together in the flesh.

Unkeepable Promises

As we think through these issues, I hope we learn to disbelieve some of the things we have come to believe about our lives and our relationships. Social media offer unkeepable promises. Now that we've exposed and explored these broken promises, in chapter 2 we'll look at those promises from a theological perspective. The Scriptures have much to say about the themes brought to light by communication theory—the importance of the body and in-the-flesh togeth-erness, boasting, and community. I was surprised at how much God's Word says; you may be, too.

The "Facebook Group"

My undergraduate career began with a four-day orientation; we were handed a rigorous schedule that we had to follow to the letter. During that week, I found my friends. As noted in the beginning of this chapter, many of them were my Facebook "friends," but we had never exchanged more than a couple wall posts back and forth. As a matter of fact, most of these people thought the way some of us were using Face-book was creepy, bordering on unhealthy.

Out of that orientation week, a dozen or so of us from the original Facebook group *did* become close, and before we knew it, we were doing everything together. We had grand ad-ventures into our new city, ate great food, and probably spent more money than we should have those first few weeks. We were loud, obnoxious, and loved every minute of it.

Early in the semester, though, a funny thing happened: other students started calling us the "Facebook group," which was ironic, because none of us had ever really spoken to each other digitally once the school semester began. Our friendships were built on a foundation of in-the-flesh togetherness and intimacy through conversation: trips to Navy Pier and Millennium Park, long hours spent "studying" (read: talking and procrastinating) in local coffee shops. The original "Facebook group," of which I had been a digital member, was scattered all over campus, victims of the promises of digital community, font-based friendships, and bodiless bonding.

DO SOMETHING

If something funny or interesting happens this weekend, try the following experiment: text one of your friends about the event, and then tell, in person, another (even if you have to wait a few hours or a day).

Which experience was better, more fun, more engaging? What role does the body play in experiencing joy? I'll answer that question for you—it plays a huge role. So do this: write your best friend or your parents a letter (a *handwritten* letter) about a special time you shared. How did being together in the flesh make a difference to your experience?

Because Facebook gives us opportunity to tell everyone everything all the time, you may be feeling lonely. That's okay—great, even. Go do something creative or fun or exciting, all by yourself, and tell no one you did it. How does it feel to have something between you and God? How does it feel to no longer broadcast yourself to the world?

Chapter 2

discern

I was lonely.

Every spring break, my school offered missions trips to the student body; every spring, dozens of students would scatter across the globe for two weeks to serve in a variety of contexts. During my undergraduate years, I traveled to England on three separate occasions to serve a lovely church in a small village near Liverpool.

Because I was used to doing ministry with my closest friends, these trips always presented me a unique and necessary challenge: serving with people I didn't choose, but whom someone else chose for me. Each of my trips to England was monumental for me—I was called to grow in new ways each time.

On my second trip, it seemed that I was to learn something about the difference between loneliness and solitude. Ten days into the trip, I was missing home, missing my friends, and longing to feel known as I am by my closest friends.

One afternoon, during some downtime, I sat in my room, gray clouds peeking into the windows of my host family's home. Robert and Mary, my host parents, were out and about, and I was home alone. I logged onto Facebook to leave a status letting everyone back home know that our trip was going well, and to update my supporters on what was happening that night at Formby Baptist Church. Before I knew it, I'd spent over an hour looking at my friends' Facebook profiles, digging through old pictures, smiling at memories that we'd shared in semesters past. At about the sixty-fifth minute of my searches, I had a realization: I had spent an hour trolling the Facebook profiles of my closest friends and family, to the exclusion of hundreds of others.

This was not the usual "stalking" trip.

In that moment, I realized that I was using Facebook as a kind of narcotic to numb my aching soul. Unable to spend time with my friends and family, I did the next best thing: I peered into my friends' lives with a kind of voyeuristic desire I'd never experienced before. I became a peeping Tom, eavesdropping into my friends' lives as a kind of substitute for being in their presence.

This was another time that I began to wonder whether Facebook really was just a simple tool, a plaything. This was when I began to wonder if Facebook and social media had a power that I hadn't expected, a power to appeal to our souls with a false balm for their pains.

Discerning Desires

Discernment is an act of the heart and the mind in which we uncover hidden motives in ourselves and in the world around us, and in so doing, begin to see the ways in which we need to change our behavior. *Discernment happens when we reflect on those things that are most true*, and then think critically and Christianly about one thing or another and, in view of these truths, live differently.

In the following pages, I want to discern the desires of our hearts that are appeased—temporarily, fleetingly, and unsatisfactorily—by social media. In short, what I am offering here is a theological treatise on social media. I am, you see, a theologian; and so are you, dear reader.[23] If you have read the Bible, if you have made a statement about the nature of God or what the Bible has to say to a certain situation, you are a theologian.

When I first started learning doctrine, I hated it. I thought it was cold, heartless, needless, and fruitless. We are a generation addicted to experience and emotion. We do not like it when such things as propositions and outlines enter into our spiritual lives—we are used to catharsis and cacophony, not the slow, quiet discipline of thinking.

I once accused theology and theologians of being terribly boring and impractical; now I see theology as the most practical thing there ever was. To a very great degree, to think rightly is to feel rightly and thus to act rightly. Our doctrine and our beliefs about God, the church, sin, salvation, and the person of Jesus act as the heartbeat that drives every part of our spiritual lives. Like our heartbeats, we often forget that they're there. Yet just as every once in a while we remember that our heartbeat is there, so every once in a while we remember what guides our practice in everyday life.

In this chapter, I'm asking, "What does the whole Bible have to say about social media?" As it turns out, it says a lot.

Fractured and Afraid

I am not sure that there is a more appropriate place to start than with sin. Sin is the constant undertow that has been dragging us out to sea since our first parents rebelled against God by eating the forbidden fruit. That single decision shattered everything about us. Most notably, it shatters our relationships. Where once there was trust, there is now deceit. Where once there was love, there is now hate. Where once there was intimacy, there is now fear. Where once there was acceptance, there is now shame. Adam and Eve lived together in harmony and unity that should have been passed on to each of us. Now we live in a world of endlessly shattered relationships.

In short: sin separates. It has broken our relationship with the Almighty and it has broken our relationships with each other. In most of Paul's listing of sin, the issues are relational: "sexual immorality, impurity, passion, evil desire, and covetousness....wrath, malice, slander, and obscene talk" (Colossians 3:5, 8).[24]

Here is where social media enter in: they prey upon our sin nature, salting wounds that we've held for centuries. "Technology is seductive when what it offers meets our human vulnerabilities," explains Sherry Turkle, director of the MIT Initiative on Technology and Self. "And as it turns out, we are very vulnerable indeed."[25] With careful reflection, we begin to see that social media actually hold to the same values that are manifested by the sin in our lives.

When we look on the scene that befell our first parents, we can easily liken them to the technological media that we have surrounded ourselves with today. Remember that when Adam and Eve ate the fruit, "the eyes of both were opened, and they knew that they were naked. And they sewed fig

unfriend yourself

leaves together and made themselves loincloths" (Genesis 3:7). In that moment, shame and fear welled in their chests as each felt overwhelmingly vulnerable before the eyes of the other. So they hid their nakedness.

We still do this today. We are constantly maneuvering and jockeying for security in our relationships; we are each too aware of our shame and vulnerability. Now, with social media, and the ability to post *this* picture, make *that* comment, and *like* that band, I can present an ideal me, and so shield myself from the disdain of my peers. The question is: are social media the new leaves we use to cover our shame? After all, "We can write the Facebook profile that pleases us. We edit our messages until they project the self we want to be."[26]

When sin came roaring into the world, it shattered the intimacy and peace we had with each other, leaving only strife. Because of it, we both long for and shrink from intimacy; we all desire to be close to another, but when the rubber hits the road, we'd rather be apart. "We are lonely but fearful of intimacy."[27] To engage in relationship after the fall is to engage in a kind of calculus of the heart in which we balance our overwhelming need for togetherness with our uncontrollable desires to flee from being known.

There is a reason we all prefer mediated communication— phones, texts, social media. It is because they are safe and

44

controlled. "In some contexts, digital communication has become the more 'natural' form of communication. It feels easier, safer, and more efficient than talking face-to-face."[28] With social media, I hide behind my computer screen, and I am shielded and protected from an unkind word or a hurtful glance. Yet this protection comes at a high price: we find ourselves disembodied, and this is a serious breach of who we are.

Living as a Person

When God created us, we were given bodies, and this is a good thing: "The Lord God formed the man of dust from the ground and breathed into his nostrils the breath of life" (Genesis 2:7). The Scriptures tell us that our bodies are "fearfully and wonderfully made" (Psalm 139:14). Bodies are important in the Scriptures—in fact, a unique feature of Christian theology is an emphasis on the body. Despite a million cartoons and TV commercials, we are not raised to everlasting life with a white robe and angel's wings, but in our own bodies *glorified,* made like Jesus' resurrection body.[29]

The body is so important to God that Jesus Christ came to us bodily (John 1:14; Colossians 1:15). We should be clued into the importance of bodies in general when we remember that Jesus is the full and final way of knowing God—and He has skin.

Our personhood is inevitably and undeniably wrapped in our physical presence, which is something Quentin Schultze suggests is absolutely necessary for communion. Yet when we move online, we leave our bodies behind, in a way, traveling to a new realm, "a world I don't inhabit."[30] In these "out-of-body experiences," we find that confusion can creep in. Any more, the lines between what happens online and what happens in real life (known by some as simply "away from keyboard") become blurred:

> The omnipresent artificiality of identity within these spaces . . . may leave some students feeling distanced, isolated, or even disconnected . . . And as we have discussed, taking experience out of the real world, divorcing it from risk and real world consequence, may have the effect of subsequently diminishing or altering its (the experience's) real world significance.[31]

The most meaningful things in our lives happen when we are embodied—it is when we live in our flesh and bones that we make memories, build friendships, and live together. Ultimately, our bodies are necessary for us to experience the truest form of another element of life affected by social media: community.

Living Together

Dietrich Bonhoeffer, in his classic *Life Together,* writes "It is not simply to be taken for granted that the Christian has the privilege of living among other Christians."[32] This is a privilege that my generation understands well—we *love* community, so much so that it's quite the buzzword among young, hipster evangelicals.

Some say that we can find community on Facebook, that social media have revolutionized the way that we experience relationships and live with one another. As Lenora Rand notes in *The Christian Century,*

> The popularity of social media sites seems to testify to the fact that many people miss what the church used to provide: a place to know others and be known, a place to weep with those who weep and laugh with those who laugh, a place to bear one another's burdens and share one another's joys, not just once a week or once a month or at Easter and Christmas, but daily. And that is what Facebook is all about: reflection and confession, support and community.[33]

While we would love to believe that social media can give us a place to "know and be known," the question is whether that can happen through mediated communication. Sure, I can read about someone's burdens and joys, but can I truly weep with those who weep when they are in their house and I am in mine? I don't think so. I can weep *for* them but certainly not *with* them.

I would argue that community, as biblically defined and God given, is not possible online. First, we have to remember that there has been a fundamental confusion about the words *network* and *community*. At the most basic level, we cannot expect community from something intended for a network. "When technology engineers intimacy, relationships can be reduced to mere connections. And then, easy connection becomes redefined as intimacy."[34]

Further, we have to ask if community is possible when, as noted earlier, social media is so based on the self. "For all the rhetoric about cyber-community, the Internet is less a forum for shared public life than an arena for individuals to express their egos and find information in tune with their personal needs and desires."[35] When the network is based on the self, it becomes incredibly difficult to "love one another earnestly from a pure heart" (1 Peter 1:22). Love "does not insist on its own way" and doesn't "boast" (1 Corinthians 13:5, 4). The hallmark value of Christian community is love: "Above all these put on love," says Paul (Colossians 3:14). Clearly, we have a problem when we seek community on a medium that is more about us than it is about others.

Oddly, though we have the highest praise for community, we are also quick to forgo it and seek community with one another behind computer screens. Bonhoeffer wrote that "it is by the grace of God that a congregation is permitted to gather visibly in this world to share God's Word and sacrament."[36] To gather "visibly" is, by necessity, to gather bodily. He wrote that "the physical presence of other Christians is a source of incomparable joy and strength to the believer,"[37] yet we would rather relate digitally—at great cost to our joy and experience of, in Bonhoeffer's words, God's very own grace.

Community has been necessarily physical since the beginning. The Scriptures say, "So God created man in his own image, in the image of God he created him; male and female he created *them*" (Genesis 1:27, emphasis mine). "As those created in the image of God, we have our personal being in interpersonal communion with God and others."[38] In the New Testament, bodily community is assumed: "And let us consider how to stir up one another to love and good works, not neglecting to meet together" (Hebrews 10:24–25a). Remember, too, that churches were instructed to greet each other with a "holy kiss" (Romans 16:16) or "the kiss of love" (1 Peter 5:14).

And here's the kicker: In 2 John, the apostle writes, "Though I have much to write to you, I would rather not use paper and ink. Instead I hope to come to you and talk face to face, so that our joy may be complete" (2 John 12). We have to keep in mind that John said this using the most advanced form of technology available to him at that point in history—a letter. At that time in history, a handwritten letter carried for miles by a messenger was the hippest, coolest form of technology there was: letter writing *was* the social network of the first century.

John recognizes that community is best experienced when we are face to face, looking each other in the eye, hearing one another's voices. He recognizes that mediated communication just isn't the same thing as in-the-flesh communion. In fact, his writing indicates something about the way the universe works: in-the-flesh, face-to-face time is how our joy is made complete.

Sociologists call the best kind of community relationships "strong ties." These are deep, meaningful relationships that motivate us to action and to change. By contrast, "the platforms of social media are weak ties."[39] While weak ties have their own kind of power, they are only effective "at increasing *participation*—by lessening the level of motivation that participation requires."[40] In short, the community on Facebook is the lazy kind. Whereas true community requires hard work ("love one another *earnestly*," writes Peter), social media provide us a kind of community that requires little of us. "In other words," writes Malcolm Gladwell, "Facebook activism succeeds not by motivating people to make a real sacrifice but by motivating them to do the things that people do when they are not motivated enough to make a real sacrifice."[41]

Yes, there is the rub—social media creates false communities that are not based on sacrifice, which is a key part of any community. My youth pastor, Paul, used to tell us when we went on trips that we needed to be "flexible," which is really another way of saying "be sacrificial." We must remember that "to be human in the image of the trinitarian God means to love others with a love that is costly and self-sacrificing."[42] I would add: to be *a community* in the image of the trinitarian God is to love others with a love that is costly and self-sacrificing.

It would seem that the God-intended way for us to experience community was selflessly and in the flesh. This is because "the companionship of a fellow Christian [is] a physical sign of the gracious presence of the triune God."[43] Here is the linchpin of why we must not seek community online: when we venture there, we miss the most important part of community, which is experiencing God as we experience one another.

Reunited

I came back after those two weeks abroad and was so glad to be home. They were by no means torturous weeks; I simply missed "my people," those who know me best. Talking to them about the trip and the events that happened during my two weeks away gave me, as John would have it, a very full joy. The best part was looking them in their eyes, embracing after a few weeks apart. *The sound of our laughter in the flesh was so much better than it was over Skype.*

It was in that moment that I realized how very necessary face-to-face relationships are. It was also in that moment that I realized there is absolutely no replacement for "the real thing." I looked to Facebook in my time away as a means to do a job it couldn't do. I was lonely and let it drive me to a strange place of need and relational desire.

I don't like Diet Coke because it just doesn't taste like the real thing—and leaves a strange, plasticky aftertaste. Sure, there have been many times that I have tried to "settle" for a Diet Coke when there is nothing else available, but I always regret that decision. I always end up getting a glass of water afterward. Online community—an oxymoron, really—is like that. It's just not as good as the real thing and leaves a gross aftertaste. At the end of the day, there is no replacement for the real thing—in-the-flesh togetherness.

DO SOMETHING

This was a shorter chapter, but hey, it's Saturday. Here are a few things to ponder:

How important is physical touch when you are lonely? Is it an important part of living in community? Find out for yourself: find someone to hug. Right now. Your roommate. Your brother. Your mom.

Have you ever been intentional about making yourself appear a certain way on Facebook? Were you covering your shame? *On Monday morning, go back and make your profile look like the real you, as scary as that may be.* I once liked about a dozen bands I'd never listened to—delete the "likes" that don't truly depict who you are.

Call your best friend, or someone you know, and ask them to go out to lunch after church tomorrow. Afterward, reflect on your experience. Was it hard to make eye contact? Was it hard to be honest and authentic? Was it better than you expected?

Chapter 3

decide

A lot of what you've read was birthed in the fall of 2010, while the leaves were turning orange and gold. I started speaking and writing at length when the weather was turning cold in Chicago. Much of what I wrote caused me to reflect on previous experiences with social media and relationships, such as my experience with the "Facebook group" when I came to college. Everything I read and wrote at that time had me feeling very strongly about social media.

If you can believe it, I was much more skeptical then— perhaps even cynical—about Facebook. I was ready to shut down my Facebook account and unfriend myself forever. I was on the brink of asking others to do the same. I was so concerned and so alarmed by what I was reading and think-ing about that I thought it best to say farewell to Facebook forever. Before I could, though, something happened. I read a book, and I started doing student ministry. The book was *Culture Making: Recovering Our Creative Calling* by Andy Crouch. When I actually started doing student ministry, I put what I read in Crouch's book into actual practice.

In January 2011, I started working with [CHaOS], the student ministries at the Village Church of Bartlett.[44] Michael (who is now one of my closest friends), the pastor at Village Church, had called a few months earlier to ask if I would be interested in coming on board at Bartlett. Long story short: I fell in love with the church and the students and decided to stay as long as Jesus and Village Church would have me.

The interesting part of stepping into ministry with middle school and high school students was that it put everything I had been studying into a very real light. I quickly learned that none of my students communicated via email—their primary means of communication with anyone was through Facebook. After only a month at Village Church, most of the students had added me as a friend. If I wanted to touch base with students during the week, I wrote on their wall or sent them a private message. I started making weekly events on Facebook and found that the number of students who responded was actually an accurate estimation of who would and would not show up to something we planned.

All of this presented me with an interesting quandary: in order to communicate with my students at all, I needed to keep my Facebook account, even though I had no real desire to keep my profile in working order. Despite my general aversion for social media, and my general desire to separate myself from it as much as possible, I found that it had quickly become a great tool when applied to its proper purposes.

I say all this to make it clear: I do not hate Facebook, and I do not think that outright abstinence from social media is the best idea. This brings us back to Crouch's work.

Condemning Condemnation

Culture Making is all about how we create change, or how we fail to create change. Crouch asserts that culture is what we make of the world, meaning "our relentless, restless human effort to take the world as it's given to us and make something else."[45] This includes "omelets, chairs, and snow angels" and so much more.[46] In essence, culture is not made of ideas or thoughts or beliefs, but stuff—or goods.

Crouch explains that there are four common ways of changing culture: condemning, critiquing, copying, and consuming.[47] Many reactions to social media are expressions of each of these approaches. In the early stages of my study, I was most eager to join the condemnation camp and be done with it.

Yet, in the end, condemnation only takes us so far. "However, if all we do is condemn culture," Crouch points out, "especially if we mostly just talk amongst ourselves, mutually agreeing how bad things are becoming—we are very unlikely indeed to have any cultural effect."[48] As I considered simply condemning social media, I realized with Crouch's help that simply saying no and shutting off my Facebook profile wouldn't do anything. Why? Because condemnation rarely leads to lasting change. This is why Crouch suggests a fifth way of engaging culture: creation.

Doing a New Thing

"The only way to change culture is to create more of it," Crouch explains.[49] "So, if we seek to change culture, we will have to create something new, something that will persuade our neighbors to set aside some existing set of cultural goods for our new proposal."[50]

In the final chapter of this little book, here is our final task: offering a new proposal to our friends (real and digital alike) that can change the way we see social media, our friendships, and ourselves. In this last chapter, we'll explore ways to cast a new vision for social media that we can start acting on *now*.

In the pages that follow, I make a handful of suggestions about how we can use social media differently, communicate wisely, and relate virtuously. That's what these are—suggestions. Not commands, not rules, but ideas that have crossed

my mind during the past year and that are drawn from
people much smarter than I, and of course, from the Scriptures. Since these are suggestions, feel free to see what you
read over the next half hour or so as a buffet—you can take
what you like and skip over what you don't. You may choose
to implement one or two of these suggestions now and add
more later. Whatever you do, don't put the book down until
you've made a decision to live differently.

In all honesty, it's my hope that at this point you've started
to sense an urgency about technology and social media, a
kind of urgency that leaves you asking, "What now?" You see,
thinking deeply is fruitless unless it leads to action. There
have been many times in studying for this project that I have
experienced "paralysis by analysis." After studying so much,
and after thinking so deeply, there have been moments when
I felt as though I had no idea what to do in light of everything
I'd come to understand. Unfortunately, many of the books I
read by cultural critics never moved from thought to action.
Postman notes that many cultural critics are "armed less with
solutions than with problems."[51] As someone who is interested, at least slightly, in the bottom line, I admit this frustrates
me to no end.

In the end, I won't tell you to close down your social media accounts; though, you may choose to do so. In the end, I am going
to suggest that we remain "in the world" but not "of the world."

Be Your Own Master

Technologies, and the ideas and media they produce, have a curious power over us. Did you know that "Facebook addiction" is searched online 350 times more than "cigarette addiction"?[52] Many people who are regular social media users have a difficult time being away from their profiles for too long.

In his book *Technopoly: The Surrender of Culture to Technology,* Postman describes how so many of us have become "technophiles," people who "gaze on technology as a lover does on his beloved, seeing it as without blemish and entertaining no apprehension for the future."[53] Technophiles are the embodiment of the technopoly, which Postman says is as much a state of mind as it is a culture.[54]

This state of mind "consists in the deification of technology, which means that the culture seeks its authorization in technology, finds its satisfactions in technology, and takes its orders from technology."[55] This last element, "takes its orders from technology," is key to understanding our relationship with social media.

More often than not, the users become the used. Much like Gollum gazing at and yearning for the ring in J. R. R. Tolkien's The Lord of the Rings trilogy, we feel a strange compulsion to gaze upon our precious profiles and treasured tweets.

Some of us find ourselves checking our Facebook profiles without thinking about it, gazing into the bright screens of our laptops and phones.

The first suggestion I offer is this: do not be the used by social media. Be the user. Paul writes, "'All things are lawful for me,' but not all things are helpful. 'All things are lawful for me,' but I will not be enslaved by anything" (1 Corinthians 6:12). *While social media like Facebook or Twitter are lawful, they are not always helpful,* and can in fact lead to slavery.

The question, of course, becomes, "How do I know that I am enslaved?" You might be addicted to social media if you check your profile in the middle of conversations, or if you update your status the moment you wake up, or if you feel antsy when you've been unplugged for a while.

Be honest with yourself: do you rule your media or do your media rule you?

Use Supplements Supplementally

I have a friend, Jonathan, who is a health nut. Unlike anyone I have ever met, Jonathan knows all about what foods are made of, what kinds of hidden chemicals are bad for your body, and what vitamins and minerals you need to experience optimal health. Jonathan also knows a fair bit about supplements— he's a self-taught expert on fish oils and extracts.

Supplements, according to Jonathan, are the key to a healthy lifestyle. They fill in the gaps left by the three meals we eat each day—that is to say, they supplement what our diets lack. But what if we only ate supplements, and never actually ate any meals? What if, instead of sitting down for meals, we started downing twenty or thirty capsules a day, forgoing regular meals?

As some of my friends like to say, "bad things." Replacing actual meals with supplements can lead to only one thing: a starving person. At the end of the day, supplements lack what our bodies need to survive: calories and other important nutrients.

Facebook is a great tool for supplementing and augmenting relationships, much in the same way fish oil is a great tool for supplementing our diets. However, many of us are replacing the main courses of our lives—in-the-flesh, face-to-face time with friends and family—with supplemental wall posts and tweets. Studies show that most of us talk to each other more online than we do in real life.[56] The forms of communication that take place through social media are not the best forms of communication. Social media act best as a "supplement to our lives."[57]

Yet, the more and more we supplement, the more and more we lose sight of what is really important. Going back to an earlier chapter, we start to confuse communication and communion. When "technology engineers intimacy, relationships can be reduced to mere connections. And then, easy connection becomes redefined as intimacy."[58]

Instead of supplementing our lives with the false intimacy provided to us by social media, we need full meals of communion and intimacy. Such meals come not from the passivity of social media, but from the intentionality of two friends sitting across cups of coffee or bowls of spaghetti.

Face-to-Face

The next suggestion is very closely tied with the last—and that is choosing to give your friends face-to-face time. It is in times like these that intimacy is born, friendships are made, and communion is cultivated.

We looked in the last chapter at how the apostle John preferred in-the-flesh communication over writing letters. "Though I have much to write to you, I would rather not use paper and ink. Instead I hope to come to you and talk face to face, so that our joy may be complete" (2 John 12). Later, he writes similarly, "I had much to write to you, but I would rather not write with pen and ink. I hope to see you soon, and we will talk face to face" (3 John 13–14).

The phrase "face to face" is, in the original languages, "mouth to mouth." This was a euphemism, a manner of speaking, that those living in John's time understood to reference what we would call communion, or "quality time."

Social media, as mediated communication, simply lack the fullness that in-the-flesh communion provides. Yet, as social media become more and more a part of our society, we are learning to forgo face-to-face communication and default back to mediated communication, which you may remember is a concession that entered into our lives as part of the sin of Adam and Eve.

Instead of allowing our relationships to be mediated, we have to choose to be face to face more often than not. This means going for coffee, playing a game, and using our words to move past communication and arrive at communion. *Looking someone in the eye is difficult—and is becoming more difficult, I think, as we learn to relate digitally.* Being honest is hard, being authentic is sometimes terrifying, and relating in the flesh is risky. Yet when we take a risk and engage in communion, we find life's simplest and profoundest pleasure: joy.

Avoid Being "Just"

"I'll just text him."

"I'll just shoot her a message."

"I'll just write on his wall."

At one point or another, we've all said a phrase like these.

And, I would wager, we've all said the same four-letter word in using such a phrase. It is this four-letter word that I would like to add to the list of those that shouldn't be said in polite conversation.

The word is *just*.

This is the word of relational deference, a curious capacity in all of us that has gained strength since the advent of social media. One of the major problems with social media is that it gives us the feeling of doing our relational responsibility, without ever actually acting on that responsibility.

A few months ago, a good friend of mine went into the hospital for a minor head injury. News of Jerell's accident spread around campus like wildfire, not only through word of mouth, but through social media as well. As this happened, we, his friends, had a choice to make: how do we let Jerell know that we are concerned and worried and praying for him?

Jerell's Facebook account exploded, with people putting comments on his wall. I visited him at the hospital, and while I was there, his phone announced that he had a new text about every twenty minutes. By the end of his hospital visit, few had visited or even called. Most people had chosen to defer relational responsibility and did the easy thing instead: they "just" texted.

When we write on a Facebook wall or send a text, it is comforting, yes. But we recognize that a text or a call isn't all there is—there is always a possibility of going even further out of our way for someone. Social media has strengthened a sinful desire we all have—to defer our relational responsibility, to fail to love earnestly (1 Peter 1:22).

I took a counseling class from a professor who is now a good friend and mentor (and an elder at my church to boot). During the class, we talked about hospital visits, and how we can best communicate with people who are hurting. To do this, he showed us the following chart.[59] Moving up from left

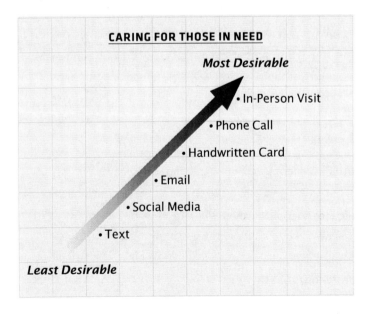

CARING FOR THOSE IN NEED

Most Desirable

• In-Person Visit
• Phone Call
• Handwritten Card
• Email
• Social Media
• Text

Least Desirable

to right, we see the least desirable forms of communication moving toward the most desirable forms of communication.

This chart helps us know if we are deferring relational responsibility. We can't go wrong by moving farther up and to the right of this chart. In light of what the apostle John wrote, the more we move to the right the more complete our joy becomes. When we move down and to the left, odds are we are deferring our relational responsibility to technology, efficiency, and selfishness.

The funny thing is that we can all accept this chart based on our experience. When you are home sick, or in the hospital, or feeling down, which of these would you prefer? A text would be nice, certainly. And who doesn't like a "get well soon" card? A phone call is nice, but when someone comes to visit you, that's the best.

As you read this chart, ask yourself, *How do I care for the people in my life? Do I tend to hover at the bottom or top of the scale?*

Filter This

Like most people in my generation, I am addicted to coffee. I am, however, a lazy addict. French pressed coffee always seems like too much work to me, so unless someone else is brewing, I'm using a good, old-fashioned coffee pot, with a filter.

Filters are handy devices. They stop the bad from getting in with the good, so when it comes to coffee, it gives us delicious coffee without any extra floaters in there. If there is anything we need on Facebook and social media, it's a filter.

You may remember this from the first chapter:

> Self-Presentation
> + Sinful Selves
> = Self-Promotion

As was explained earlier, the social media have an agenda—and that agenda is to get us to talk about ourselves a lot. Social media do not tend to have godliness, holiness, and righteousness as values—as such, they do not hinder us from becoming full-blown narcissists trumpeting the minor details of our lives to the world.

What we need, then, are filters to guide our posting, our tweeting, and our updating. The Scriptures provide a few. The first is found in Ephesians 4:29, "Let no corrupting talk come out of your mouths, but only such as is good for building up, as fits the occasion, that it may give grace to those who hear."

A difficult question to ask when I am posting on social media is this: Will what I write here build someone up? Will it give them grace, the fuel on which our spiritual lives run? Or, is what I am writing slanderous? Malicious? Boastful?

Another filter can be found in Matthew: "I tell you," Jesus says, "on the day of judgment, people will give account for every careless word they speak" (12:36). As someone who has, as I put it, "a lot of words," I find this verse terrifying. In light of social media's drive for us to text and tweet and post endlessly, it should give us pause to wonder how many careless words we have spoken. I have read and written many a post that was glib, quick, and even hurtful. Along these lines we must remember that the Scriptures tell us to be "slow to speak" (James 1:19) and that "whoever guards his mouth preserves his life" (Proverbs 13:3).[60]

For a third filter, remember that we are to think in a certain way: "Finally, brothers, whatever is true, whatever is honorable, whatever is just, whatever is pure, whatever is lovely, whatever is commendable, if there is any excellence, if there is anything worthy of praise, think about these things" (Philippians 4:8). Thinking inevitably leads to action—so we need to think the right way in order to speak (and by extension, post and tweet) the right way. Look over some of your posts: are they good? Honorable? Praiseworthy? Such questions will help put that third filter correctly in place.

Out of Your Excess

In the same passage in which we find that we are going to be judged for our careless words, Jesus says that "out of the abundance of the heart the mouth speaks. The good person out of his good treasure brings forth good, and the evil person out of his evil treasure brings forth evil" (Matthew 12:34b–35). It is important to understand that the excess of our heart is not discovered, usually, in the way we speak when we're thinking about it. The excess of our heart is revealed by what we say flippantly, thoughtlessly, in the moment. (I frequently know the condition of my heart by how sarcastic and cynical I am—because it is my sense of humor that represents, in part, the excess of my heart.) If you chose to, you could get a very real sense of where my heart is by reading my Facebook profile.

Our use of social media reveals so much about us. Because Facebook and Twitter are so rooted in the immediate, and because we tend to post multiple times each day, our profiles begin to act as collectors for our hearts' excess. This actually can be a good thing: our social media profiles, which we so often forget are public, create immediate accountability. What we say is broadcast to possibly hundreds, and over time, what we broadcast can reveal heart attitudes and motives that need to be addressed.

Blessed Skepticism

My critics, since I first began researching this project, have called me cynical, skeptical, and old-fashioned.[61] On many levels, I can accept each of these accusations, especially the accusation regarding skepticism. On some level, the Scriptures encourage us to live in a kind of skepticism, watchfulness, and caution.

It's called wisdom, or maybe, blessed skepticism.

Paul writes, "Look carefully then how you walk, not as unwise but as wise, making the best use of the time, because the days are evil" (Ephesians 5:15–16). We live in wicked times and are called to dwell in "the world," which has a system of values that are generally diametrically opposed to those held by the people of God.

The Scriptures tell us to "test everything" (1 Thessalonians 5:21). As we've said, we cannot, like the technophiles, "gaze on technology as a lover does on his beloved, seeing it as without blemish and entertaining no apprehension for the future."[62] Instead, we are to maintain, as God's people, a great apprehension for the future, and seek in earnest to find blemishes in our technologies. Why? Because we are called to a blessed skepticism. Postman writes that we must be "resistance fighters" to the technological takeover of the world.[63] He explains that "a technological resistance fighter maintains… [a] distance from any technology, so that it always appears somewhat strange, never inevitable, never natural."[64]

My hope is that we would become a generation that embodies what it is to live in blessed skepticism of new technologies and new media. The social media revolution, Facebook and

Twitter and the like, includes powerful cultural forces that are shaping the way we see the world and how we believe we should live and relate. It ought not to be met with unquestioning attitudes, but with questions of wisdom and skepticism. We should always question our technologies; doubt is never a bad place to start when it comes to these sorts of things.

All Things for Christ

People who disagree with my critique of social media often quote Colossians 1:15–16: "He is the image of the invisible God, the firstborn of all creation. For by Him all things were created, in heaven and on earth, visible and invisible, whether thrones or dominions or rulers or authorities—all things were created through Him and for Him."

"Look," they say, "all things were created by Christ and for Christ, so we need not fear these media." To a degree, I'm with them.

John Piper uses this very reasoning to explain why he has chosen to tweet. He writes that he tries "to fill these media with as much provocative, reasonable, Bible-saturated, prayerful, relational, Christ-exalting, truth-driven, serious, creative pointers to true greatness" as he can.[65] He conceives of tweets as opportunities "to press some God-focused truth into someone's consciousness."[66]

Many arguments in favor of social media tend to be pragmatic; some spin an "it works, so do it" way of thinking. Piper has resisted this kind of thinking. Of all of the arguments in favor of social media as a tool for glorifying God, it is Piper's that I have consistently found the most compelling. "But it seems to us," he says, "that aggressive efforts to saturate a media with the supremacy of God, the truth of Scripture, the glory of Christ, the joy of the gospel, the insanity of sin, and the radical nature of Christian living is a good choice for some Christians."

I cannot help but agree. *Perhaps the greatest filter of all is asking the question: Is what I am posting glorifying to God?* Does it fill this medium with the truth of Scripture? The glory of Christ? This principle would guide us well, as it has Piper—and a few other users[67] who consistently encourage the church to love Jesus more through their 140-character posts.

Skeptical Glorifiers

Our goal is not to be condemning—our goal is to be creating, and to walk wisely as we do. Here is how we can change the world of social media: by using social media skeptically in order to glorify God and put Jesus on display. Will it save the nations? I doubt it.[68] But it will make Jesus more famous and that is the best goal to have; after all, it is the goal of the entire universe.

Yes, I agree with Piper. But, again, blessed skepticism is the order of the day. We have to hold in tension that "sin is crouching at the door" (Genesis 4:7) and that we live under "this present darkness" (Ephesians 6:12). This is why we must remember the words of the Scriptures—that we are called to be *in* the world but not *of* the world (see 1 John 2:15–16). We are *of* our Father, manifesting His values and His kingdom as we proclaim the gospel to every creature; yet we act on these values and embody His kingdom *in* the world, which opposes Him and, by extension, us. We can bow to this opposition, and so become world-*ly* or we can resist it, through blessed skepticism, through wisdom. "Euphoria over information technology is a secular faith that deserves heretics," writes Quentin Schultze. "Unless we see this idol for what it is, we will becomes its servants. Distrusting high-tech idols is a noble task and a cosmic responsibility."[69]

My hope is that we become a generation that questions technology, that chooses to fight for friendships and relationships, and that seeks to use these ever-more-present technologies as opportunities to glorify God. Social media is a great tool—a tool we must subdue, and not be subdued by.

DO SOMETHING

So there are a lot of things to think about. What are the top three that you can put into action right away?

1._____

2._____

3._____

Do your media run you, or do you run your media? Here's how you can answer that question: track how much time you spend on social media every day. How many minutes do you spend? How many times do you check your Facebook account? This week, cut your use by half.

At the end of the weekend, how does it feel to be apart from your media? Some people feel anxious, jittery, and worried. Some feel disconnected and alone. How has it been being "unplugged" for so long?

How can you offer your friends and neighbors a better way to use Facebook? Do you think this will have any lasting change? Why or why not?

Conclusion

There. You did it. Three days away from Facebook and Twitter and Foursquare. Was it difficult?

It's all right if it was—and if you cheated a little. I'm positive that almost everyone who reads this book will log on at least once during the weekend, either because they instinctively check their profiles when they wake up, or because they need to get some info from a friend, or simply because they don't care what I say.

That's okay with me.

My hope for you is that you have thought, and thought deeply, about this thing that is at our fingertips and before our faces so frequently. My hope is that you have experienced what I experienced after first reading about these things: a sense of panic, of urgency. I hope you are in some way compelled to at least think differently, to pause before posting.

My hope in writing this book is not that people would unfriend themselves indefinitely, closing their profiles and ending their accounts. My hope is that people would say farewell to what we've allowed Facebook to create—a new kind of social and intellectual environment that encourages false intimacy and feigned friendship.

My hope is that we would be a people who remember what it is to live in the flesh, to dwell face to face with each other, and to live virtuously online. My hope is that we become a people who remember that we are created in God's image, and so created as a community ("male and female he created *them*").

My hope is that we become conversers, listeners, huggers, hearers, smilers, lookers-in-the-eyes—friends, essentially.

Afterword

October 17, 2011

Only a few days ago, I asked my best friend to marry me. Much to my joy, she said yes.

Like so many couples do, we spent a few hours on the phone with those we love and those who love us, to tell them the good news. We heard many screams and laughs and congratulations. Then, after the phone calls were done, we took one final step.

Stephanie and I changed our Facebook profiles from "In a Relationship" to "Engaged." Then, a curious thing happened: over the next twenty-four hours, a photo I'd posted collected over 125 likes, and over fifty comments. Our "changed relationship status" received nearly a hundred likes, and dozens of comments. We each found our profiles covered with con-gratulations, encouragements, and notes from friends.

When Steph and I returned to Chicago a few days after the Facebook frenzy, we had a very important realization: telling people of our engagement over Facebook was not nearly as fun as telling people in the flesh. It was fun to watch people grab her hand to get a closer look at the ring. It was fun to receive hugs and smiles. It was fun to tell our story in person instead of over the phone.

One year ago I began to suspect that social media were subtly robbing us of something; exactly one year later, I know very well what is being stolen from us: joy. We didn't experience joy because of the many likes and comments. We experienced something *like* joy, in the same way a photo-graph of a sunset is *like* a sunset. It wasn't until we saw each other face to face, until we greeted each other in the flesh that we found joy, joy robbed from us by digital expressions of congratulations and excitement.

So, dear reader, remember that in our use of social media, something great and important is at stake: our joy.

Notes

1. Harry Blamires, *The Christian Mind: How Should a Christian Think?* (Vancouver, B.C.: Regent College Publishing, 2005), 3. Thank you to the good doctors O'Neal and Johnson for putting this book into my hands, and into my mind, and in so doing, totally changing my life.

2. Ibid., 18.

3. Tim Challies, *The Next Story: Life and Faith After the Digital Explosion* (Grand Rapids: Zondervan, 2011), 14.

4. For the record (and this is something that I had to practice) *media* is the plural form of the singular *medium*. Tell your friends. You'll look smart.

5. Nicholas Carr, *The Shallows: What the Internet Is Doing to Our Brains* (New York: W. W. Norton, 2011), 3.

6. Neil Postman, *Amusing Ourselves to Death: Public Discourse in the Age of Show Business*, 20th anniversary ed. (New York: Penguin , 2006), 84.

7. Ibid., 83.

8. Carr, *The Shallows*, 3.

9. Ibid.

10. Postman, *Amusing Ourselves to Death*, 84.

11. Ibid., 87.

12. Ibid., 91.

13. Libby Copeland, "The Anti-Social Network," *Slate*, January 26, 2011, http://www.slate.com/id/2282620/ (accessed August 6, 2011).

14. It is for this reason that some think that Facebook and other social media may lead to depression. See "Is Social Media Ruining Students?" Online Schools, http://www.onlineeducation.net/social-media-and-students (accessed August 6, 2011). Also, Alexander H. Jordan et al., "Misery Has More Company Than People Think: Underestimating the Prevalence of Other's Negative Emotions," *Personality and Psychology Bulletin* 37, no. 120 (2011): 120–35. Granted, the evidence is split pretty evenly about social media's connection to depression or low self-esteem. See Soraya Mhedizadeh, "Self-Presentation 2.0: Narcissism and Self-Esteem on Facebook," *Cyberpsychology, Behavior, and Social Networking* 13, no. 4 (2010): 357–64. One more: Amy L. Gonzales and Jeffrey T. Hancock, "Mirror, Mirror on my Facebook Wall: Effects of Exposure to Facebook on Self-Esteem," *Cyberpsychology, Behavior, and Social Networking* 14, no. 1–2 (2011): 79–83.

15. "Obsessed with Facebook," Online Schools, http://www.onlineschools.org/blog/facebook-obsession/ (accessed August 6, 2011).

16. Carr, *The Shallows*, 85.

17. Sherry Turkle, *Alone Together: Why We Expect More from Technology and Less from Each Other* (New York: Basic Books, 2011), 11.

18. Quentin Schultze, *Habits of the High-Tech Heart: Living Virtuously in the Information Age* (Grand Rapids: Baker, 2004),167.

19. Ibid.,175.

20. Turkle, *Alone Together*,153.

21. Ibid., 12.

22. Challies, *The Next Story,* 92. Italics original.

23. And, as so many of my dear professors have taught me, we all are. *Everyone* is a theologian, Dr. Bryan O'Neal taught me in my first theology class. It's just a matter of whether we are good theologians or bad theologians.

24. See also Romans 1:28–32, 1 Corinthians 6:9–10, and so many more.

25. Turkle, *Alone Together,* 1.

26. Ibid., 12.

27. Ibid., 1.

28. Challies, *The Next Story,* 77.

29. See Philippians 3:20–21, 1 Corinthians 15:20, 23.

30. This is the brilliant title of a brilliant journal article: Stuart Boon and Christine Sinclair, "A World I Don't Inhabit: Disquiet and Identity in Second Life and Facebook," *Educational Media International* 46, no. 2 (June 2009): 99–110.

31. Ibid., 108.

32. Dietrich Bonhoeffer, *Life Together: The Classic Exploration of Faith in Community,* first ed. (New York: HarperOne, 1978), 17.

33. Lenora Rand, "The Church on Facebook: Why We Need Virtual Community," *The Christian Century* 126, no. 13 (2009): 22–25.

34. Turkle, *Alone Together,* 16.

35. Schultze, *Habits,* 180. Further, "Instead of renewing community, these ever expanding cybernetic systems tend to band people together in like-minded or similarly interested groups. They equip us with new means of pursuing our own interests more than they nurture communities of diverse people who nevertheless seek shared lives and common ends."

36. Bonhoeffer, *Life Together,* 18.

37. Ibid., 19.

38. Brad Harper and Paul Louis Metzger, *Exploring Ecclesiology* (Grand Rapids: Brazos, 2009), 42.

39. Malcolm Gladwell, "Small Change," *The New Yorker*, October 4, 2010, http://www.newyorker.com/reporting/2010/10/04/101004fa_fact_gladwell.

40. Ibid.

41. Ibid.

42. Harper and Metzger, *Exploring Ecclesiology*, 156.

43. Bonhoeffer, *Life Together*, 20.

44. [CHaOS] is an acronym for "Christ Has Annihilated Our Sins." Just so you know, dear reader, I get to work with the best group of students that exist in the world. I love them dearly.

45. Andy Crouch, *Culture Making: Recovering Our Creative Calling* (Downers Grove, Ill.: InterVarsity, 2008), 23.

46. Ibid., 23.

47. Ibid., 68–69.

48. Ibid., 68.

49. Ibid., 67.

50. Ibid., 67. Crouch later notes that "human nature abhors a cultural vacuum. It is the rare human being who will give up some set of cultural goods just because someone condemns them. They need something better, or their current set of cultural goods will have to do, deficient as they may be. . . . No matter how much we may protest—condemning the cultural goods on offer—unless we offer an alternative, the show will go on." See Crouch, *Culture Making*, 68.

51. Neil Postman, *Technopoly: The Surrender of Culture to Technology* (New York: Vintage, 1993), 182. Postman writes, "Anyone who practices the art of cultural criticism must endure being asked, What is the solution to the problems you describe? Critics almost never appreciate this question, since, in most cases, they are entirely satisfied with themselves for having posed the problems and, in any event, are rarely skilled in formulating practical suggestions about anything." See p. 181.

52. "Obsessed with Facebook," Online Schools, http://www.onlineschools. org/blog/facebook-obsession/ .

53. Postman, *Technopoly*, 5.

54. Ibid., 71.

55. Ibid.

56. "Obsessed with Facebook," Online Schools.

57. Challies, *The Next Story*, 92.

58. Turkle, *Alone Together*, 16.

59. This chart is derived from a class lecture given by Mike Boyle, Assistant Professor of Pastoral Studies at the Moody Bible Institute in Chicago.

60. The book of Proverbs has a wealth to say on speaking and staying silent. See Proverbs 12:23, 14:3, 15:4, 15:7, 15:28, 17:27–28, 18:7, 18:21, 20:19, 21:23. These are just a few of the many—but all of them help us when it comes to creating a new social media culture.

61. These are the critiques of most people under age thirty. Those who are over forty tell me this project is needed, helpful, and wise. Who is right? Maybe both.

62. Postman, *Technopoly*, 5.

63. Ibid., 182.

64. Ibid., 185.

65. John Piper, "Why and How I Am Tweeting," The Desiring God Blog, entry posted June 9, 2009,http://www.desiringgod.org/resource-library/taste-see-articles/why-and-how-i-am-tweeting (accessed August 6, 2011). John Piper's handle is @JohnPiper.

66. John Piper, "How Do I Think About Tweeting? - a Response to John Mayer," The Desiring God Blog, entry posted July 25, 2011, http://www.desiring-god.org/blog/posts/how-do-i-think-about-tweeting-a-response-to-john-mayer (accessed August 6, 2011).

67. I have been encouraged and edified by Rick Warren's tweets (@rickwarren).

68. That said, I'm open to anything. Someone reading this could tell me that a tweet or a friend's Facebook post played an integral part of the decision to cross the line of faith—and for that I am thankful. I'm suggesting that this will not become the norm for evangelism, and shouldn't.

69. Schultze, *Habits*, 195-96.

Acknowledgments

This is a short book, but that doesn't mean writing it was a short process. What you are reading is product of over a year's worth of reading, writing, speaking, conversing, listening, and researching.

I must first thank my professors, because they gave me the skills that helped me create this book. My professors taught me to think and write and read, and so they deserve many thanks. Thank you, especially, Brian Kammerzelt, for talking about this for hours on end; thank you, also, to the two dozen professors who first heard my presentation and said, "This is good."

Next, I owe great thanks to David Ulrich for listening to me talk about this project, coming to the first presentation, and then believing in it so much that he made it his pet project and pitched it to Moody Publishers. David is one of the most inspiring individuals I know, and his projects are going to be far more revolutionary than mine could ever be. Visit him at sackclothandtea.com.

I love Moody Bible Institute, and I love Moody Publishers. It is fitting that my first book be published through the place I love so much. Thank you Randall, Duane, and Brandon for editing, marketing, and making this happen.

Many of my friends heard me talk about this for hours on end—thanks to Joshua and Travis who pushed me to make this book theologically accurate and rhetorically clear. Thank you, Neal, for researching this with me for ACSD, and to Luke, Jerell, Bob, Pam, Mike, Lindsey, Carly, Ashley, Dr. deRosset, and Michael for coaching me on. Thank you James, for coming up with the name of chapter 3. Thanks to the Manvalanche for encouraging me to keep researching as I was in the midst of graduation and everything else.

Thank you, Steph, for being you, for so many encouragements, and for letting me be absent so I could write. Thanks for almost doing cartwheels in Third Coast when we found out the book was accepted.

Much love and gratitude to Village Church of Bartlett. Thanks for helping me realize my heart's desires—ministry and writing—so early on. To my students, I love you very dearly.

Thanks to my parents for letting their little boy trade in the basketball for pen and paper. Thanks for freeing me to do what I am good at, and preventing me from any further embarrassment that could have been garnered in athletics. Thanks, Mom, for being my first editor, and teaching me to love reading and writing.

Finally, I have so much gratitude to God, who gave me a desire to write so long ago, and is now letting me fulfill this desire. "I will sing to the Lord, for He has dealt bountifully with me."

THE MESSAGE BEHIND THE MOVIE

ISBN-13: 978-0-8024-3201-8

Too often, Christian books expose the underlying messages in Hollywood films without equipping believers to discuss those messages and to use them as springboards for sharing the gospel. In a fun and approachable style, movie lover and apologetics professor Douglas M. Beaumont enables all who enjoy movies to watch wisely, thus engaging the culture without disengaging their faith.

MOODY
PUBLISHERS
www.MoodyPublishers.com

THE COFFEE HOUSE CHRONICLES

ISBN-13: 978-0-8024-8768-1

ISBN-13: 978-0-8024-8766-7

ISBN-13: 978-0-8024-8767-4

With over 40 million books sold, bestselling author Josh McDowell is no stranger to creatively presenting biblical truth. Now, partnering with fellow apologist Dave Sterrett, Josh introduces a new series targeted at the intersection of story and truth.

The Coffee House Chronicles are short, easily devoured novellas aimed at answering prevalent spiritual questions. Each book in the series tackles a long-contested question of the faith, and then answers these questions with truth through relationships and dialogue in each story.

MOODY
PUBLISHERS

www.MoodyPublishers.com

ALL IN

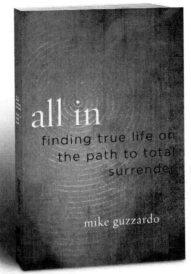

all in

finding true life on the path to total surrender

mike guzzardo

ISBN-13: 978-0-8024-1783-1

All In is designed to help readers overcome what may be the greatest problem facing so many of us today—the lack of a genuine experience with God. Tapping into the widely felt need of spiritual dissatisfaction, gifted author and speaker Mike Guzzardo guides you along the path of total surrender to Jesus Christ. He tells great stories that will lead you to experience your own story, for better or worse, and he helps to open your eyes to how a genuine encounter with God will irrevocably change your whole life.

MOODY
PUBLISHERS

www.MoodyPublishers.com

IMAGINE THAT

ISBN-13: 978-0-8024-2450-1

Drawn from his own experiences performing Mozart, playing "dive bars," and leading worship and arts in the church, author Manuel Luz explores the questions that Christian artists often ask. His thought-provoking journey through the convergence of art and faith will draw artists closer to the One they imitate, knowingly or unknowingly, in every creative endeavor.

MOODY PUBLISHERS

www.MoodyPublishers.com

THINGS I WISH I KNEW

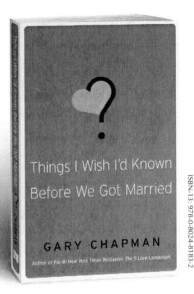

This is not a book simply to be read. It is a book to be experienced.
The material lends itself to heart-felt discussions by dating or
engaged couples. To jump-start the exchanges, each short chapter
includes insightful "Talking it Over" questions and suggestions. And,
the book includes information on interactive websites as well as
books that will enhance the couples' experience.

NORTHFIELD
PUBLISHING

www.MoodyPublishers.com